Snap Back:
Ten Steps
To Snap Back
After They've Left!

Jonita G. Saint-Leger

Copyright © 2012 Jonita G. Saint-Leger

All rights reserved.

ISBN-13:9780615837475

DEDICATION

The light of God surrounds us;
The love of God enfolds us;
The power of God protects us;
The presence of God watches over us.
Wherever we are, God is.
And all is well.

CONTENTS

ACKNOWLEDGMENTS

Thank you for the teachers, the lessons and the supporters. I have been blessed with those who have looked my way and with confidence, told me to "do you! I have full confidence in you."
Never a doubt in my dreams, never a naysay from their mouths. It takes a world of life experience to be able to know those who truly have your back. I think I've lived that.
Thank you to Changa K. Rose, My four music makers, Kamili, Solomon, Korin and Samara. Thank you to my mother Benedita Hill, Tabitha Washington, Ayana Mbonu, Angelique Edwards Cooper, Greer Marshall, Keya Jacobs and Walter T. Mudu.
Thank you for the continued love of my siblings, Fernando Hill, Regina Hill, Akindeji Hill, and Schandell Hill

Life is a wonderful thing and I thank all who share in mine and make each day a reason to live and a reason to give.

Prologue

I was taught that the light of God came through me, surrounded me and protected me and I believed it. My faith was sealed. I was a part of God and God was in me. I knew that the universe was made up of what most couldn't understand. It was the unanswered questions, the sense that there was more and the unshakeable feeling that somehow, I had a mystical effect on the outcome of my own experiences.

That feeling lived in the family of childhood innocence and imagination. The same realm that spoke of miracles, dreams and philosophical theories.
Though these were childhood thoughts they strengthened the faith in me that my will alone, was enough to make great things happen.

The problem with growing up is that we lose the will and the understanding that we are able to do great things and instead concentrate on the mundane events of the every day. We say that we believe in God but forget our own powers blessed by God. We allow our light to be dimmed by our surroundings and accept the punishments doled out by the world in the natural as truth to what we deserve and who we are.

In my case, my light was dimmed at the very start of my marriage and I hadn't realize it. I became oppressed. There were now rules and expectations of being a wife that I hadn't yet understood, never mind accepted. I truly believed that in loving me, my husband had accepted me part and parcel and that no changes to my person were necessary. It seems, that expectations were ingrained in him. His past perceptions of what a wife was, had ingrained itself in our story and was trying to shape me into the women in his family that he knew growing up.

The problem not realized by either of us was that in most of those instances, those marriages ended in divorce and children outside of the marriage. I should have seen it then with his attempts to change me but was blind. My own past references of my parent's marriage told me that you stay in a marriage "no matter what!"

I was raised to believe that relationships are constantly changing, people are constantly growing and that there are many stages to a marriage. This I have learned to all be true; the problem, was that I hadn't realized that these changes and growth should occur in a happy healthy marriage, not one that is struggling and limping to get along.

I kept waiting for it to get better. My own expectations were that we would "get" to that happy place, that in time we would shape our relationship like a well fitted glove, my spouse didn't feel the same. He felt that our glove was one made of steel and he couldn't make it fit nor bear the weight.

I am a strong advocate for marriage, I believe in the strength of the marital bond and I believe in the force of a family. What I didn't realize was that there was an exit clause that could be utilized.

Catching up with an old friend on the phone one day, he shared with me his recent life events and I congratulated him on the marriage that I had read posts about and followed on his social media page. I was surprised when he told me that it was over. It had been annulled quick as a flash when a deal breaker occurred. As much as he loved her and valued what they had, he knew that what occurred in their marriage at the start was a precursor to something bigger and he was already on marriage number two, he had learned from the first and would not repeat his mistakes.

Almost a year into the marriage he took advantage of the annulment clause and ended it.
I was shocked at this revelation. There were events that happened on my honeymoon that should have done the same for me, but this was my first marriage and I was in it for the long haul, it had never occurred to me that an annulment was an option.

What's the worst that could happen? As is said, "if you love someone set them free, if they return they were always yours, if not, they never were." Now a year later after the annulment my friend and his ex for the second time worked out their issues and remarried. In their case, the return ensured a desire to have the proper building blocks in place, and a desire to nurture their relationship.

Divorce can be ugly, annulment is a chance to rip the bandage off and let yourself heal. Divorce can also be a series of slow pokes in a festering wound, requiring much more for the healing to occur. For me, annulment was not an option, I instead, was faced with divorce. This is my story of how my healing began.

1

BELIEVE IT

When It Happens Believe It. It had to be the biggest shock in my life, to be told that all of the time that I invested in my marriage would have no long-term reward other than that of our four children. There was strong disbelief that in fact it had ended. There would be no graduations of grandchildren together, there would be no retiring to tour foreign lands together. There would be no moments sitting side by side reminiscing about the journey that we shared together, instead it was ending in divorce.

It is a death and your entire life together and that of which you planned flashes in your mind in an instant. "This can't be real, this can't be happening," but when your eyes once again regain focus and you then find the face of your spouse initiating this unexpected conversation you realize that it is actually happening, and this person, really wants out.

Don't crack, literally! This is not said lightly. There are more than enough examples of people who have fallen to drugs and alcohol immediately after being abandoned. It's an easy fix, but it's a slippery slope not easily recovered from.

If you have children, remember that they need you. If you don't, remember that YOU need YOU. Don't let things get out of control. This is a vulnerable time in your life and the vultures will circle around you. There will always be someone willing to hand you a drink, a pill, a "smoke," a needle or their pillow and pimp you out, figuratively and literally. It's extreme, but it's real. You have to remember who you are, who you've decided you want to be and be

THAT person. Don't let anyone, this or any situation define you.

2

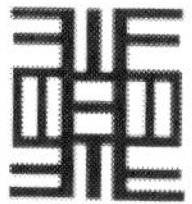

Denying Denial

A person in denial, doesn't know it. Their reality is completely as they fashion it. Realizing that you are in denial is like pulling yourself from a dream and realizing that it was "just" a dream. While in it, all that you think and feel seems instinctual, real, a feeling to trust, but it's not, it's denial.

This is when you must trust your brain, your ears, your eyes and trust the actions that you are witnessing. You may feel that he/she will return, know it to be true in your heart but his/her actions are contrary. There are no personal phone calls, there are no personal visits, there are no warm moments unless you have opened a door that says "use me." and in those moments, that is all that it is.
If there are the infamous words "one day," "someday" and "soon" in terms of reconciling, you need to see what work is happening now! Are the two of you in couples counseling, a marriage ministry or any individualized counseling to right the wrongs of your relationship? If not, then it's just talk and "one day", "someday" and "soon" will never come. It is time to move on. Close that chapter and heal the you that at this time may seem fragmented. It's about you and your creator. You were not created the day you were married, you already were. Go back to your source and be the perfect being that the universe created.

Know that the departure of your mate is based on their reality, their experiences and their choices, not yours. That is their story to tell, know your truth! Don't worry about the joint friends, families and colleagues. Yes, they are all important, but they too will make their own choices, your truth will set you free. You will know quickly who's in your corner, who's not and who's neutral, and none of it is your choice to make. Focus on what you can do for yourself. This time is all about healing you. This is the time for you to start a new story. Why not make it a good one?

3

HOLD ON TO YOU

Never let go of the you, you envisioned yourself to be. What was it you envisioned for yourself before the marriage? Have you accomplished the goals you once set for yourself? If not, get back to work! If so, let's take it to another level! Remind yourself on those hard days that show up to pull yourself together, do not allow yourself to fold and crack no matter how much it hurts; especially if you have children.

Understand that self-pity is like quicksand, you've got a small window of time to get yourself out of it, otherwise, the suction will just pull you down until you're suffocated. Give yourself that small window to grieve wholeheartedly and then close that door and pull yourself up and out!

The whole science around divorce is schizophrenic! The day I took my ex back to court for enforcement of child support is the day our oldest daughter became a young lady and received her menses. This was a big day for our daughter. We raised her to be comfortable enough to come to us with anything and when this happened unlike myself who sheepishly told my mother and then begged her not to tell my father or any other soul on the planet, our daughter shouted it from the peak of the mountain. She called her father and let him know the news, she spoke with his side of the family, my side of the family and it was an event.

Though the outcome of the court actions that day could have resulted in him being arrested I felt the need to connect with him regarding our daughter. Knowing that he may have resentment towards me was of no consequence, I was no longer going to have him, or anyone control my actions based on their thoughts and behavior. With this in mind, I texted him. I congratulated him on us raising a young lady and asked him to continue to be there for her. That every female wants to be "Daddy's little girl." I know that her relationship or lack thereof with him will play a part in her need to be accepted by other men, so like it or lump it, this is the hand I've been dealt.

Did he respond? No, still I did me and I was able to sleep well and wake up refreshed not having held on to any anger or negative feelings regarding our relationship. The best gift that I ever received from him was truly learning to be me.

4

SELF-ASSESSMENT

Give yourself a self-assessment. Acknowledge your mental and physical health. Pay attention to your body and any stress signals given off, (are you eating too much or not at all, is your hair falling out, are you sleeping too much or not at all, are you ignoring your hygiene etc.?)

Take heed not to overexert yourself if there is any sign of physical distress (every time I spoke to my ex, with the usual exchange of vitriol, I broke out with hives (I am talking from the top of my head to the tip of my toes!) If you find that your mental disposition is not what it usually is, take note. Are you leaking your situation to strangers (this is not necessarily a bad thing and can lead to self-awareness, but if your leaking uncontrollably, you need to reel yourself in and find a counselor whose duty it is to listen.)

Are you unable to carry out day to day duties? Assess yourself and look for ways to get the support that you need ie. contact divorce support groups by way of churches, community organizations, hospitals, and individual groups.

This is a death that you are experiencing, and your pain and grief are real. Do not deny yourself the right to express this pain but be healthy about it. There is no shame in getting help. The problems come if you deny yourself and try to handle it alone.

Get the help you need and then get back into your life and do what you do best. Remind yourself what that is. See the greatness in you. If you are an artist, create, if you are a business person, work your business to its fullest possibilities, just make sure, that you keep yourself focusing on things that you can control.

The marriage is over and out of your hands, and you and your life will go on. Now what are you going to do about creating the life that you DO want?

5

READING IS FUNDAMENTAL

Echart Tolle and his book,"A New Earth," changed my life. I read other books as well that ranged from Don Miguel Ruiz's, "The Four Agreements," to Steve Harvey's, "Act Like A Lady, Think Like a Man." I "ate the meat and spit out the bones." There was wisdom and straight talk found in these books and good advice was what I was in need of most of all. Friends were there to comfort me, but had trouble finding the right words. Even if they had, my denial would have caused me to ignore them. The words of an unbiased "expert," was exactly what I needed.

Forgiveness is healing, learning that the problems in the relationship were largely a result of individual baggage, unrelated to you specifically but more so to the history behind him/her is kismet. We are the reflection of our experiences, we are the reflection of the experiences of others (our family/past relationships). We cannot know all that our parents, teachers, leaders or mates have encountered in their lives. We cannot know what reflection of others shaped them and then in turn shaped us.

What we can learn is that they are all personal journeys and we are not vessels meant to contain all of their baggage. We must let it stand where it lies and work diligently to creating a healthy future where their experiences and expectations do not define who YOU are.   All of the above came to me from reading Echart Tolle's "A New Earth." This book was my saving grace, find yours.

6

KNOW YOUR WORTH

"To the world you may be one person but to one person you may be the world."

– Dr. Seuss

There is someone in the world who needs someone just like you. I'm not talking romantically - yet. You can certainly be of service to someone. Find a cause that you believe in, join with a belief in yourself and you will find that other's will believe in you. There are plenty of charities that you will find that will enjoy your much-needed participation. The best part of working with a charity is working with people who all stand for the same cause with love in their hearts and good will towards those who aid the cause. You will do yourself and the world, a world of good.

Also, know this to be true, that at the bare minimum know that you are one with the creator and you have a right, a duty to believe in yourself. Be good to yourself. Memorize and recite positive affirmations. Drown out the negative words and actions of others, once again, they do not define you!

You were born with the power of greatness, you define you! You taught yourself to walk, talk, hold a spoon, learn your language, manipulate your extremities properly, assess the situations around you all with a developing brain. Now that you are developed there is no limit to what you can do, what you can become or what you can produce.

7

DISCOVER YOUR PASSION

We've talked about moving forward, being of use to others, following and completing your past goals and now we will delve just a little deeper on what makes us tick. Your passion, what is it? Have you explored your innermost joy activators? What stimulates you? If you could look into your brain, what receptors would ignite your pineal gland? It is OK not to know, but not OK to continue not to know. You're nursing a wounded heart and a wounded mind, but it is time to reawaken who you are and who you are meant to be.   What is it that stimulates you to the point of happiness and a sense of purpose? Maybe you haven't delved into the experience yet, but let's consider what gets you to your happy place that is solely reliant on your actions and your joy. Ask yourself this question and answer without prejudice or judgment of yourself.

Write out the question and the answers without hesitation. Just go and let go! Write every thought that pops into your head whether it's something you have done or never have done, write it down. See yourself in the words you write. Are you a poet, a scientist, a botanist, a boutique owner, a painter, a house painter, what do you see for yourself?

If you had a genie, what would you ask for? Who would you ask to be? It is never too late to redefine who you know yourself to be. We evolve, and so should your life choices. This is YOUR life, own it!

"Love what you do and do what you love. Don't listen to anyone else who tells you not to do it. You do what you want, what you love. Imagination should be the center of your life."

— Ray Bradbury

8

THE MARRIAGE DIED, YOU DIDN'T

(My Father always told me, "One monkey don't stop no show!") Know that relationships end AND begin. Give yourself permission to love again and to be loved in the way that you deserve to be loved.

There will be a time when you will have the desire for company once again. When is it too soon?   It is probably too soon when you are still suffering the loss of your spouse. Once you have rediscovered who you are without the marriage, once you can honestly say that you love yourself more than what you had in the marriage, once you can wish well for your ex-spouse, you are ready to move on.

If you have not yet reached this stage, give yourself more time. You are more likely to repeat the problems that existed in your marriage with a new partner if you have not yet acknowledged the wrongs and rights of your previous marriage. If you have not yet come to terms with the role you played and if you are secretly wishing that they will still come back, then you cannot yet expect to move forward.

Heal yourself before you hurt an innocent bystander. Your timetable for this to happen is yours. Don't compare yourself to others who were in your shoes. For some it will happen rather quickly, for others it may take many months or even years.

9

DO THE CHILDREN HAVE A SAY?

Your children are your biggest priority. Include them in your process. Don't wait until you can't live without him/her, to find out that your children can't stand him/her!) The most controversial aspect of dating after divorce is when is it too soon to introduce a child to a potential new mate. My answer comes from the author/radio/talk show host, Steve Harvey who suggests, that once you feel that you have met someone that you are seriously interested in and think that you can potentially start a new life with, then let him/her meet the children.

Get a feel for whether it's forced, natural or what the children's instincts tell them. Don't wait to fall in love just yet before introducing the children, you are more likely to put your wants before their needs if you work in that order.

Let the children sense his intentions and report to you their feelings. As you may have already learned, the spouse may be there temporarily, but your children are permanent. They are very much a part of the process and must be considered.

I took my own advice with my children and shared the new experience of meeting someone with them. After feeling like I met someone that might be worth getting to know better in the romantic sense, I spoke to my children about the possibility of my dating them. We discussed what it meant to them and to me to consider the company of someone other than their father. They understood that this had no bearing on their relationship with their father and that this was a new stage in all of our lives. They accepted this new step and agreed to meet the person who might make their mother happy. After they met him we went through many stages of comfortability for the children. There was the initial stage of meeting someone who had an interest in their mother, the stage of watching Mommy laugh with a man who wasn't their father, the stage of being around someone else outside in the world, the stage of Mommy holding someone else's hand, etc… through each stage, I paid attention to my children's observations, comments and feelings. This was serious business and I didn't take it lightly. We decided together that he was the man for us. After six months they accepted him as Mommy's new partner and loved him as much as I did.

10

LEAVE THE PAST IN THE PAST

Don't Allow Your Old Relationship to Rule Your New One. If you have followed steps one through nine, you have built yourself up to be the person you were meant to be. You are stronger, more grounded, more in love with yourself then you have been in a long time. Now it's time to successfully let someone new love you too.

He/she is not your old mate. If you are seeing similarities, it may be time to take a new assessment and consider what it is about you that attracts this energy. You may not yet be ready to move on. If it's that you have a "type," then consider if you are strong enough to be in a relationship with that "type" without losing who you have built yourself to be.

Give yourself an honest chance. Remember that your new relationship is a new start, an opportunity to have the relationship that you desire and deserve. As a rule of thumb, remember that all relationships are a series of negotiations. If you are on the losing end and are finding that you are constantly making concessions or demanding concessions, then you are already losing ground.

Don't worry, this can be turned around. Just as when negotiating with a supervisor or a client, there is often a fragile line and a possibility of desperation that if the relationship ends, you have lost an asset and future opportunities. This is the thought pattern you need to walk away from.

This is the time when faith steps in and reminds you of your worth. Once you are confident in who you are, your true intentions and your true desire, you must trust that the right situation and relationship will show up in your life.

Bring that assured person to the conversation and you may find that the same new relationship that started to flounder in the way of the old, gets a new wind, gets new direction and can now be built on this solid ground. If this doesn't happen, trust enough to know that the right relationship is waiting for you, and step away knowing your worth. Your successful relationship is eminent.

The day that I was no longer in denial and realized that my marriage was over was the day that I knew the right relationship was waiting for me. The thought was so strong I literally heard the sound of thunder following the thought. It was as if I had written it into my future and written it across the sky.

I moved forward into my new life getting used to being a single mother, releasing the resentment of becoming a statistic, and worked myself through the stages of one to nine. One day, I found myself doing something that I had not done in years. I was humming, whistling and dancing around my house. I hadn't even realized that I had stopped once I was married.

The day I heard my own humming, I stopped in the recognition that I was happier than I had been in years!

There was no new relationship at this time, just the relationship I renewed with myself, and it was a good one! A few months after that, the right relationship showed up and has been a blessing in my life since then.

I end this with an affirmation, that you too will love your life again. You will love yourself again, and the right person will love the person that you were always meant to be. Be well and be blessed!

Andinkra Symbols and Their Meanings

"Linked Hearts" – Understanding Agreements

"he who does not know can know from learning" knowledge,
life-long education

"talons of the eagle" bravery, strength

"I change or transform my life" bravery, strength

'wisdom knot" wisdom, ingenuity, intelligence and
patience.

"he who wants to be king" service, leadership

"snake climbing the raffia tree"   steadfastness, prudence, diligence

"the ladder of death" Mortality

"if your hands are in the dish" democracy, pluralism

"RETURN AND GET IT" LEARN FROM THE PAST

ABOUT THE AUTHOR

Jonita G. Saint-Leger is a proud mother of four. She lives in Spring Hill Fl. A native of New York, Jonita keeps New York close to her heart as her home away from home. As a Children's author, she was inspired to lead writing workshops at her children's school, she has since created a writing program that reaches children all over the world. She continues to write children books, is an English teacher, blogger, poet and advocate of youth for dropout prevention. Please visit her website at http://www.royalwriters.org

Made in the USA
Coppell, TX
29 October 2025

62058113R00018